HAL•LEONARD

Jazz Play Along®

Book and CD for B♭, E♭, C and Bass Clef Instruments

JAZZ/BLUES

9 FAVORITE TUNES

Volume 73

Produced by Mark Taylor
Arranged by Mark Taylor
and Jim Roberts

BOOK

<table>
<tr><th>TITLE</th><th colspan="4">PAGE NUMBERS</th></tr>
<tr><th></th><th>C Treble Instruments</th><th>B♭ Instruments</th><th>E♭ Instruments</th><th>C Bass Instruments</th></tr>
<tr><td>Break Out the Blues</td><td>4</td><td>16</td><td>28</td><td>40</td></tr>
<tr><td>Gee Baby, Ain't I Good to You</td><td>6</td><td>18</td><td>30</td><td>42</td></tr>
<tr><td>I'll Close My Eyes</td><td>5</td><td>17</td><td>29</td><td>41</td></tr>
<tr><td>Movin' Along (Sid's Twelve)</td><td>8</td><td>20</td><td>32</td><td>44</td></tr>
<tr><td>Night Lights</td><td>10</td><td>22</td><td>34</td><td>46</td></tr>
<tr><td>Reunion Blues</td><td>9</td><td>21</td><td>33</td><td>45</td></tr>
<tr><td>The Serman</td><td>12</td><td>24</td><td>36</td><td>48</td></tr>
<tr><td>Sunny</td><td>13</td><td>25</td><td>37</td><td>49</td></tr>
<tr><td>This Here</td><td>14</td><td>26</td><td>38</td><td>50</td></tr>
</table>

CD

<table>
<tr><th>TITLE</th><th>CD Track Number Split Track / Melody</th><th>CD Track Number Full Stereo Track</th></tr>
<tr><td>Break Out the Blues</td><td>1</td><td>2</td></tr>
<tr><td>Gee Baby, Ain't I Good to You</td><td>3</td><td>4</td></tr>
<tr><td>I'll Close My Eyes</td><td>5</td><td>6</td></tr>
<tr><td>Movin' Along (Sid's Twelve)</td><td>7</td><td>8</td></tr>
<tr><td>Night Lights</td><td>9</td><td>10</td></tr>
<tr><td>Reunion Blues</td><td>11</td><td>12</td></tr>
<tr><td>The Serman</td><td>13</td><td>14</td></tr>
<tr><td>Sunny</td><td>15</td><td>16</td></tr>
<tr><td>This Here</td><td>17</td><td>18</td></tr>
<tr><td>B♭ Tuning Notes</td><td></td><td>19</td></tr>
</table>

ISBN-13: 978-1-4234-2616-5
ISBN-10: 1-4234-2616-9

HAL•LEONARD®
CORPORATION

7777 W. BLUEMOUND RD. P.O. BOX 13819 MILWAUKEE, WI 53213

Visit Hal Leonard Online at
www.halleonard.com

JAZZ/BLUES

Volume 73

Produced by Mark Taylor
Arranged by Mark Taylor and Jim Roberts

Featured Players:
Graham Breedlove-Trumpet
John Desalme-Saxophones
Tony Nalker-Piano
Jim Roberts-Bass

HOW TO USE THE CD:

Each song has <u>two</u> tracks:

1) Split Track/Melody

Woodwind, Brass, Keyboard, and **Mallet Players** can use this track as a learning tool for melody style and inflection.

Bass Players can learn and perform with this track – remove the recorded bass track by turning down the volume on the LEFT channel.

Keyboard and **Guitar Players** can learn and perform with this track – remove the recorded piano part by turning down the volume on the RIGHT channel.

2) Full Stereo Track

Soloists or **Groups** can learn and perform with this accompaniment track with the RHYTHM SECTION only.

BREAK OUT THE BLUES

WORDS AND MUSIC BY
GEORGE SHEARING

C VERSION

I'LL CLOSE MY EYES

CD

5 : SPLIT TRACK/MELODY
6 : FULL STEREO TRACK

C VERSION

BY BUDDY KAYE
AND BILLY REID

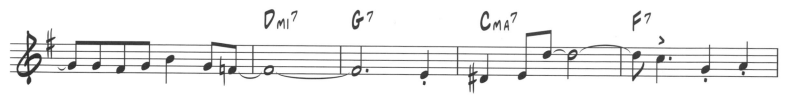

Gee Baby, Ain't I Good To You

WORDS BY DON REDMAN AND ANDY RAZAF
MUSIC BY DON REDMAN

C VERSION

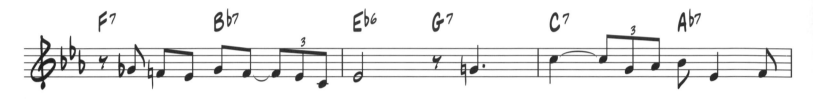

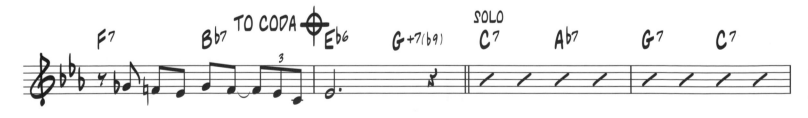

MOVIN' ALONG
(SID'S TWELVE)

BY JOHN L. "WES" MONTGOMERY

C VERSION

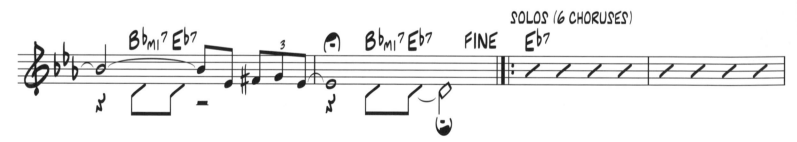

REUNION BLUES

CD
◆11 : SPLIT TRACK/MELODY
◆12 : FULL STEREO TRACK

BY DUKE ELLINGTON

C VERSION

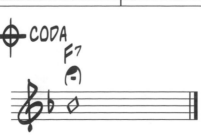

NIGHT LIGHTS

CD
◆ 9 : SPLIT TRACK/MELODY
◆ 10 : FULL STEREO TRACK

LYRIC BY SAMMY GALLOP
MUSIC BY CHESTER CONN

C VERSION

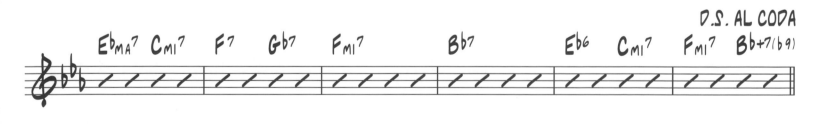

THE SERMAN

CD
🔳13: SPLIT TRACK/MELODY
🔳14: FULL STEREO TRACK

C VERSION

BY HAMPTON HAWES

Sunny

WORDS AND MUSIC BY
BOBBY HEBB

THIS HERE

WORDS BY JON HENDRICKS
MUSIC BY BOBBY TIMMONS

WITH - IN YOUR_ HEART THAT REALLY IS WHERE YOU FIND IT._____

TO CODA ⊕

SOLOS

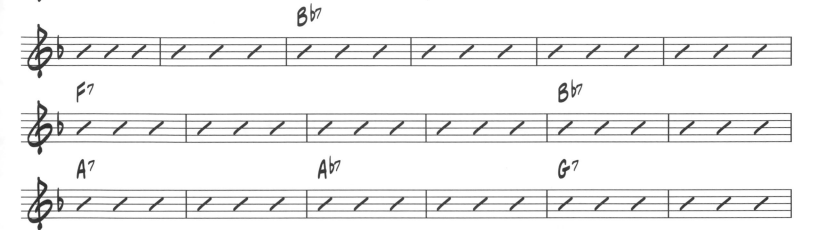

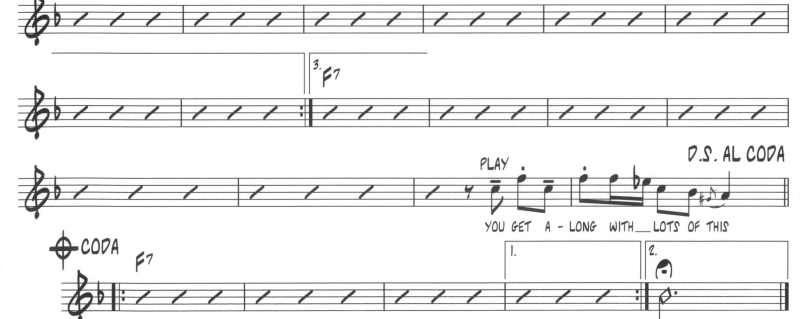

PLAY

D.S. AL CODA

YOU GET A - LONG WITH__ LOTS OF THIS

⊕ CODA

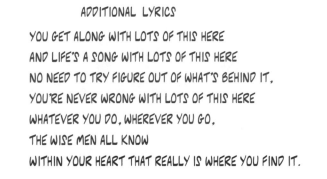

ADDITIONAL LYRICS

YOU GET ALONG WITH LOTS OF THIS HERE
AND LIFE'S A SONG WITH LOTS OF THIS HERE
NO NEED TO TRY FIGURE OUT OF WHAT'S BEHIND IT.
YOU'RE NEVER WRONG WITH LOTS OF THIS HERE
WHATEVER YOU DO, WHEREVER YOU GO,
THE WISE MEN ALL KNOW
WITHIN YOUR HEART THAT REALLY IS WHERE YOU FIND IT.

CD

1 : SPLIT TRACK/MELODY
2 : FULL STEREO TRACK

BREAK OUT THE BLUES

WORDS AND MUSIC BY
GEORGE SHEARING

B♭ VERSION

MEDIUM SWING
N.C.

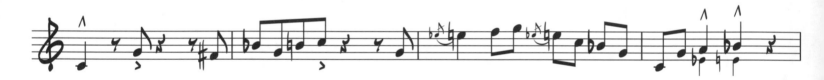

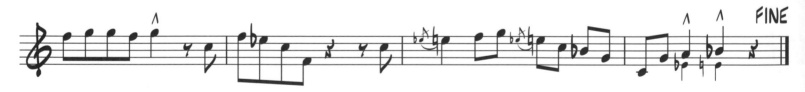

I'LL CLOSE MY EYES

CD
5: SPLIT TRACK/MELODY
6: FULL STEREO TRACK

BY BUDDY KAYE
AND BILLY REID

Bb VERSION

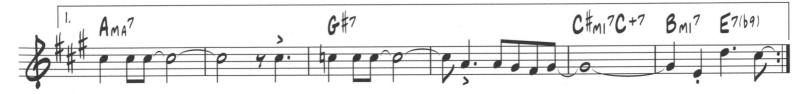

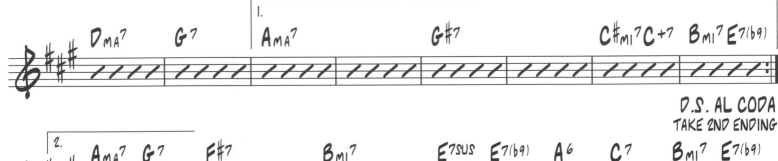

CD
3 : SPLIT TRACK/MELODY
4 : FULL STEREO TRACK

Gee Baby, Ain't I Good to You

WORDS BY DON REDMAN AND ANDY RAZAF
MUSIC BY DON REDMAN

Bb Version

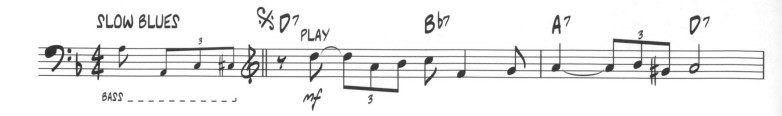

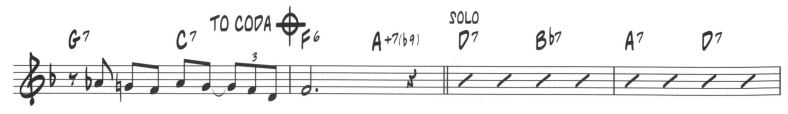
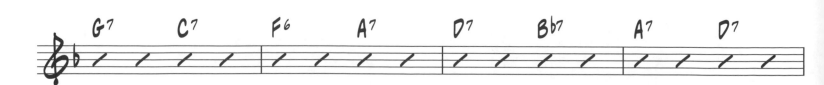

MOVIN' ALONG
(SID'S TWELVE)

BY JOHN L. "WES" MONTGOMERY

B♭ VERSION

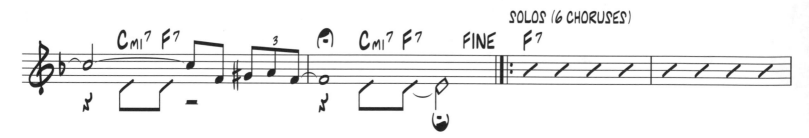

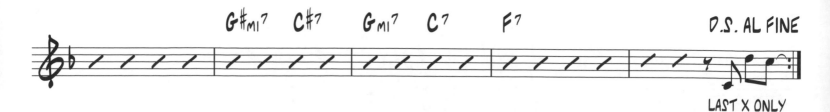

Reunion Blues

BY DUKE ELLINGTON

Bb VERSION

NIGHT LIGHTS

LYRIC BY SAMMY GALLOP
MUSIC BY CHESTER CONN

CD

THE SERMAN

BY HAMPTON HAWES

B♭ VERSION

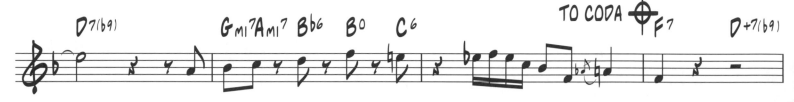

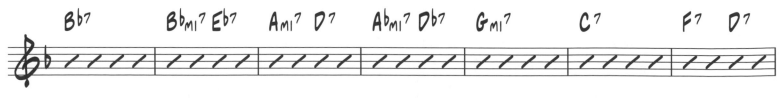

Sunny

WORDS AND MUSIC BY
BOBBY HEBB

This Here

WORDS BY JON HENDRICKS
MUSIC BY BOBBY TIMMONS

WITH - IN YOUR__ HEART THAT REALLY IS WHERE YOU FIND IT._____

TO CODA ✛

SOLOS

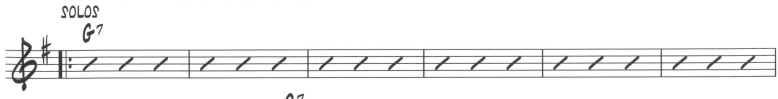

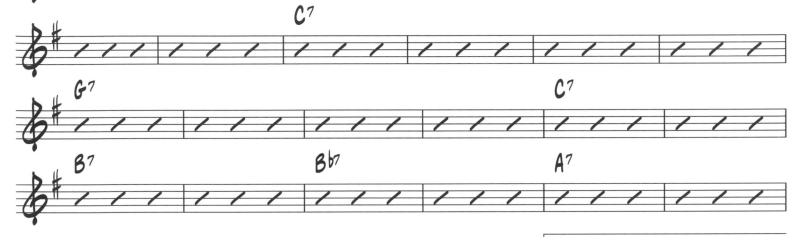

PLAY

D.S. AL CODA

YOU GET A - LONG WITH__ LOTS OF THIS

✛ CODA

ADDITIONAL LYRICS

YOU GET ALONG WITH LOTS OF THIS HERE

AND LIFE'S A SONG WITH LOTS OF THIS HERE

NO NEED TO TRY FIGURE OUT OF WHAT'S BEHIND IT,

YOU'RE NEVER WRONG WITH LOTS OF THIS HERE

WHATEVER YOU DO, WHEREVER YOU GO,

THE WISE MEN ALL KNOW

WITHIN YOUR HEART THAT REALLY IS WHERE YOU FIND IT.

BREAK OUT THE BLUES

WORDS AND MUSIC BY
GEORGE SHEARING

I'LL CLOSE MY EYES

BY BUDDY KAYE
AND BILLY REID

E♭ VERSION

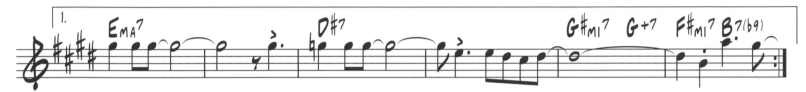

CD
3: SPLIT TRACK/MELODY
4: FULL STEREO TRACK

Gee Baby, Ain't I Good To You

WORDS BY DON REDMAN AND ANDY RAZAF
MUSIC BY DON REDMAN

E♭ VERSION

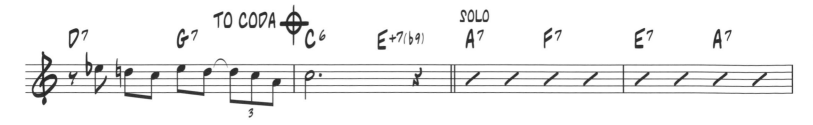

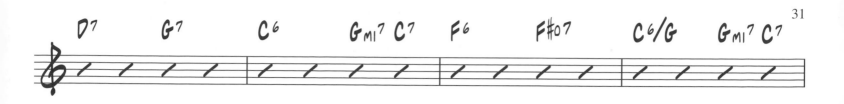

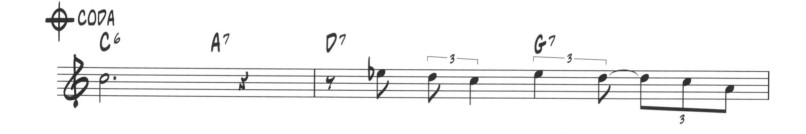

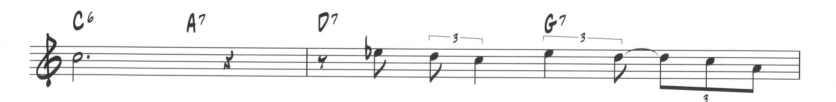

MOVIN' ALONG
(SID'S TWELVE)

BY JOHN L. "WES" MONTGOMERY

E♭ VERSION

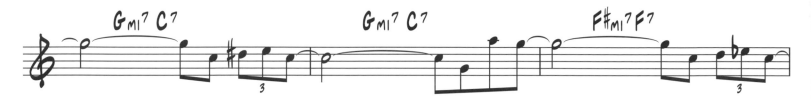

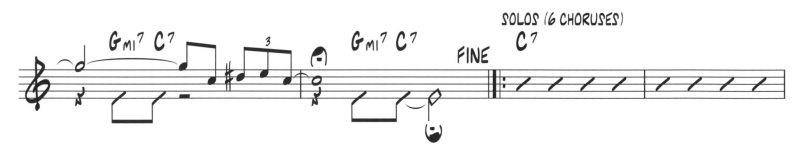

REUNION BLUES

BY DUKE ELLINGTON

E♭ VERSION

MEDIUM SWING

TO CODA ✛

RIT. LAST X ONLY

SOLOS (8 CHORUSES)

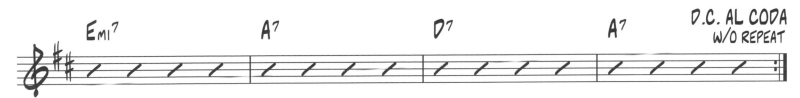

D.C. AL CODA
W/O REPEAT

✛ CODA

NIGHT LIGHTS

LYRIC BY SAMMY GALLOP
MUSIC BY CHESTER CONN

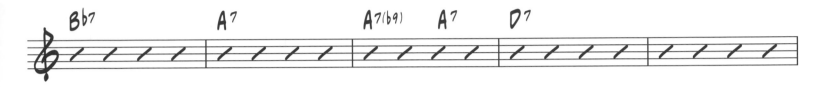

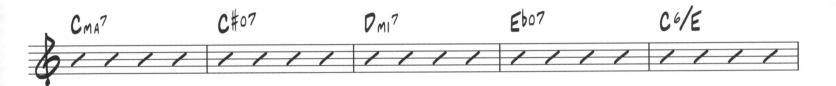

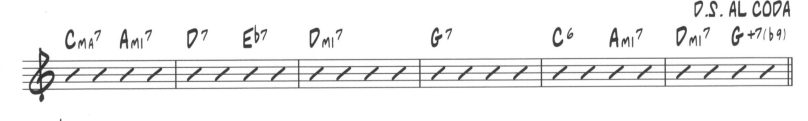

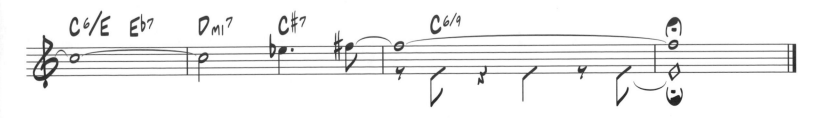

THE SERMAN

By Hampton Hawes

Eb VERSION

Sunny

WORDS AND MUSIC BY
BOBBY HEBB

This Here

WORDS BY JON HENDRICKS
MUSIC BY BOBBY TIMMONS

ADDITIONAL LYRICS

YOU GET ALONG WITH LOTS OF THIS HERE

AND LIFE'S A SONG WITH LOTS OF THIS HERE

NO NEED TO TRY FIGURE OUT OF WHAT'S BEHIND IT,

YOU'RE NEVER WRONG WITH LOTS OF THIS HERE

WHATEVER YOU DO, WHEREVER YOU GO,

THE WISE MEN ALL KNOW

WITHIN YOUR HEART THAT REALLY IS WHERE YOU FIND IT.

BREAK OUT THE BLUES

WORDS AND MUSIC BY
GEORGE SHEARING

CD
5 : SPLIT TRACK/MELODY
6 : FULL STEREO TRACK

I'LL CLOSE MY EYES

BY BUDDY KAYE
AND BILLY REID

𝄢 : C VERSION

CD
➤ : SPLIT TRACK/MELODY
◄ : FULL STEREO TRACK

𝄢 : C VERSION

Gee Baby, Ain't I Good To You

WORDS BY DON REDMAN AND ANDY RAZAF
MUSIC BY DON REDMAN

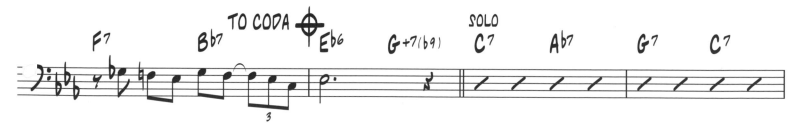

MOVIN' ALONG
(SID'S TWELVE)

BY JOHN L. "WES" MONTGOMERY

𝄢: C VERSION

REUNION BLUES

BY DUKE ELLINGTON

NIGHT LIGHTS

LYRIC BY SAMMY GALLOP
MUSIC BY CHESTER CONN

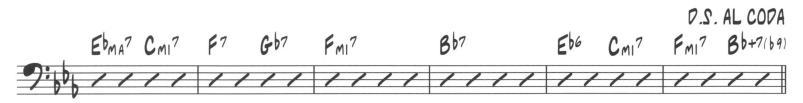

Sunny

WORDS AND MUSIC BY
BOBBY HEBB

THIS HERE

WORDS BY JON HENDRICKS
MUSIC BY BOBBY TIMMONS

51

WITH - IN YOUR___ HEART THAT REALLY IS WHERE YOU FIND IT.___

TO CODA

SOLOS

PLAY

D.S. AL CODA

YOU GET A - LONG WITH__ LOTS OF THIS

CODA

ADDITIONAL LYRICS
YOU GET ALONG WITH LOTS OF THIS HERE
AND LIFE'S A SONG WITH LOTS OF THIS HERE
NO NEED TO TRY FIGURE OUT OF WHAT'S BEHIND IT,
YOU'RE NEVER WRONG WITH LOTS OF THIS HERE
WHATEVER YOU DO, WHEREVER YOU GO,
THE WISE MEN ALL KNOW
WITHIN YOUR HEART THAT REALLY IS WHERE YOU FIND IT.

DUKE ELLINGTON Vol. 1
Caravan • Don't Get Around Much Anymore • In a Sentimental Mood • Perdido • Prelude to a Kiss • Satin Doll • Take the "A" Train • and more.
00841644.................................$15.95

MILES DAVIS Vol. 2
All Blues • Blue in Green • Four • Half Nelson • Milestones • Nardis • Seven Steps to Heaven • So What • Solar • Tune Up.
00841645.................................$15.95

THE BLUES Vol. 3
Billie's Bounce • Birk's Works • C-Jam Blues • Freddie Freeloader • Mr. P.C. • Tenor Madness • Things Ain't What They Used to Be • and more.
00841646.................................$15.95

JAZZ BALLADS Vol. 4
Body and Soul • Here's That Rainy Day • Misty • My Funny Valentine • The Nearness of You • Polka Dots and Moonbeams • and more.
00841691.................................$15.95

BEST OF BEBOP Vol. 5
Anthropology • Donna Lee • Doxy • Epistrophy • Lady Bird • Oleo • Ornithology • Scrapple from the Apple • Woodyn' You • Yardbird Suite.
00841689.................................$15.95

JAZZ CLASSICS WITH EASY CHANGES Vol. 6
Blue Train • Comin' Home Baby • Footprints • Impressions • Killer Joe • St. Thomas • Well You Needn't • and more.
00841690.................................$15.95

ESSENTIAL JAZZ STANDARDS Vol. 7
Autumn Leaves • Lullaby of Birdland • Stella by Starlight • There Will Never Be Another You • When Sunny Gets Blue • and more.
00843000.................................$15.95

ANTONIO CARLOS JOBIM AND THE ART OF THE BOSSA NOVA Vol. 8
The Girl from Ipanema • How Insensitive • Meditation • One Note Samba • Quiet Nights of Quiet Stars • Slightly Out of Tune • and more.
00843001.................................$15.95

DIZZY GILLESPIE Vol. 9
Birk's Works • Con Alma • Groovin' High • Manteca • A Night in Tunisia • Salt Peanuts • Tour De Force • Woodyn' You • and more.
00843002.................................$15.95

DISNEY CLASSICS Vol. 10
Alice in Wonderland • Cruella De Vil • When You Wish upon a Star • You've Got a Friend in Me • Zip-a-Dee-Doo-Dah • and more.
00843003.................................$15.95

RODGERS AND HART FAVORITES Vol. 11
Bewitched • Dancing on the Ceiling • Have You Met Miss Jones? • I Could Write a Book • The Lady Is a Tramp • My Romance • and more.
00843004.................................$15.95

ESSENTIAL JAZZ CLASSICS Vol. 12
Airegin • Ceora • The Frim Fram Sauce • Israel • Milestones • Nefertiti • Red Clay • Satin Doll • Song for My Father • Take Five.
00843005.................................$15.95

JOHN COLTRANE Vol. 13
Blue Train • Countdown • Cousin Mary • Equinox • Giant Steps • Impressions • Lazy Bird • Mr. P.C. • Moment's Notice • Naima.
00843006.................................$15.95

IRVING BERLIN Vol. 14
Blue Skies • How Deep Is the Ocean • I've Got My Love to Keep Me Warm • Steppin' Out with My Baby • What'll I Do? • and more.
00843007.................................$14.95

RODGERS & HAMMERSTEIN Vol. 15
Do I Love You Because You're Beautiful? • It Might as Well Be Spring • My Favorite Things • Younger than Springtime • and more.
00843008.................................$14.95

COLE PORTER Vol. 16
Easy to Love • I Concentrate on You • I've Got You Under My Skin • It's All Right with Me • It's De-Lovely • You'd Be So Nice to Come Home To • and more.
00843009.................................$15.95

COUNT BASIE Vol. 17
All of Me • April in Paris • Blues in Hoss Flat • Li'l Darlin' • Moten Swing • One O'Clock Jump • Shiny Stockings • Until I Met You • and more.
00843010.................................$15.95

HAROLD ARLEN Vol. 18
Ac-cent-tchu-ate the Positive • Come Rain or Come Shine • I've Got the World on a String • Stormy Weather • That Old Black Magic • and more.
00843011.................................$14.95

COOL JAZZ Vol. 19
Bernie's Tune • Boplicity • Budo • Conception • Django • Five Brothers • Line for Lyons • Walkin' Shoes • Waltz for Debby • Whisper Not.
00843012.................................$15.95

CHRISTMAS CAROLS Vol. 20
Away in a Manger • Greensleeves • Hark! The Herald Angels Sing • Joy to the World • O Little Town of Bethlehem • Silent Night • more.
00843080.................................$14.95

RODGERS AND HART CLASSICS Vol. 21
Falling in Love with Love • Isn't it Romantic? • Manhattan • My Funny Valentine • This Can't Be Love • Thou Swell • Where or When • and more.
00843014.................................$14.95

WAYNE SHORTER Vol. 22
Children of the Night • ESP • Footprints • Juju • Mahjong • Nefertiti • Nightdreamer • Speak No Evil • Witch Hunt • Yes and No.
00843015.................................$14.95

LATIN JAZZ Vol. 23
Agua De Beber • Chega De Saudade • Manha De Carnaval • Mas Que Nada • Ran Kan Kan • So Nice • Watch What Happens • and more.
00843016.................................$16.95

EARLY JAZZ STANDARDS Vol. 24
After You've Gone • Avalon • Indian Summer • Indiana • Ja-Da • Limehouse Blues • Paper Doll • Poor Butterfly • Rose Room • St. Louis Blues.
00843017.................................$14.95

CHRISTMAS JAZZ Vol. 25
The Christmas Song (Chestnuts Roasting on an Open Fire) • I'll Be Home for Christmas • Let It Snow! Let It Snow! Let It Snow! • Silver Bells • and more.
00843018.................................$15.95

CHARLIE PARKER Vol. 26
Au Privave • Billie's Bounce • Donna Lee • My Little Suede Shoes • Ornithology • Scrapple from the Apple • Yardbird Suite • and more.
00843019.................................$16.95

GREAT JAZZ STANDARDS Vol. 27
Fly Me to the Moon • How High the Moon • I Can't Get Started with You • Speak Low • Tangerine • Willow Weep for Me • and more.
00843020.................................$14.95

BIG BAND ERA Vol. 28
Air Mail Special • Christopher Columbus • In the Mood • Jersey Bounce • Opus One • Stompin' at the Savoy • Tuxedo Junction • and more.
00843021.................................$14.95

LENNON AND McCARTNEY Vol. 29
And I Love Her • Blackbird • Come Together • Eleanor Rigby • Let It Be • Ticket to Ride • Yesterday • and more.
00843022.................................$16.95

BLUES' BEST Vol. 30
Basin Street Blues • Bloomdido • Happy Go Lucky Local • K.C. Blues • Sonnymoon for Two • Take the Coltrane • Turnaround • Twisted • and more.
00843023.................................$14.95

JAZZ IN THREE Vol. 31
Bluesette • Jitterbug Waltz • Moon River • Tennessee Waltz • West Coast Blues • What the World Needs Now Is Love • Wives and Lovers • and more.
00843024.................................$14.95

BEST OF SWING Vol. 32
Alright, Okay, You Win • Cherokee • I'll Be Seeing You • Jump, Jive an' Wail • On the Sunny Side of the Street • Route 66 • Sentimental Journey • and more.
00843025.................................$14.95

SONNY ROLLINS Vol. 33
Airegin • Alfie's Theme • Biji • The Bridge • Doxy • First Moves • Here's to the People • Oleo • St. Thomas • Sonnymoon for Two.
00843029.................................$14.95

ALL TIME STANDARDS Vol. 34
Autumn in New York • Bye Bye Blackbird • Call Me Irresponsible • Georgia on My Mind • Honeysuckle Rose • Stardust • The Very Thought of You • more.
00843030.................................$14.95

BLUESY JAZZ Vol. 35
Angel Eyes • Bags' Groove • Bessie's Blues • Chitlins Con Carne • Mercy, Mercy, Mercy • Night Train • Sweet Georgia Bright • and more.
00843031.................................$14.95

HORACE SILVER Vol. 36
Doodlin' • The Jody Grind • Nica's Dream • Opus De Funk • Peace • The Preacher • Senor Blues • Sister Sadie • Song for My Father • Strollin'.
00843032.................................$14.95

BILL EVANS Vol. 37
Funkallero • My Bells • One for Helen • The Opener • Orbit • Show-Type Tune • 34 Skidoo • Time Remembered • Turn Out the Stars • Waltz for Debby.
00843033.................................$16.95

YULETIDE JAZZ Vol. 38
Blue Christmas • Christmas Time Is Here • Merry Christmas, Darling • The Most Wonderful Time of the Year • Santa Claus Is Comin' to Town • and more.
00843034.................................$14.95

"ALL THE THINGS YOU ARE" & MORE JEROME KERN SONGS Vol. 39
All the Things You Are • Can't Help Lovin' Dat Man • A Fine Romance • Long Ago (And Far Away) • The Way You Look Tonight • Yesterdays • and more.
00843035.................................$14.95

BOSSA NOVA Vol. 40
Black Orpheus • Call Me • A Man and a Woman • Only Trust Your Heart • The Shadow of Your Smile • Watch What Happens • Wave • and more.
00843036 ....$14.95

CLASSIC DUKE ELLINGTON Vol. 41
Cotton Tail • Do Nothin' Till You Hear from Me • I Got It Bad and That Ain't Good • I'm Beginning to See the Light • Mood Indigo • Solitude • and more.
00843037 ....$14.95

GERRY MULLIGAN FAVORITES Vol. 42
Bark for Barksdale • Dragonfly • Elevation • Idol Gossip • Jeru • The Lonely Night (Night Lights) • Noblesse • Rock Salt a/k/a Rocker • Theme for Jobim • Wallflower.
00843038 ....$16.95

GERRY MULLIGAN CLASSICS Vol. 43
Apple Core • Line for Lyons • Nights at the Turntable • Song for Strayhorn • Walkin' Shoes • and more.
00843039 ....$16.95

OLIVER NELSON Vol. 44
The Drive • Emancipation Blues • Hoe-Down • I Remember Bird • Miss Fine • Stolen Moments • Straight Ahead • Teenie's Blues • Yearnin'.
00843040 ....$15.95

JAZZ AT THE MOVIES Vol. 45
Baby Elephant Walk • God Bless' the Child • The Look of Love • The Rainbow Connection • Swinging on a Star • Thanks for the Memory • and more.
00843041 ....$14.95

BROADWAY JAZZ STANDARDS Vol. 46
Ain't Misbehavin' • I've Grown Accustomed to Her Face • Make Someone Happy • Old Devil Moon • Small World • Till There Was You • and more.
00843042 ....$14.95

CLASSIC JAZZ BALLADS Vol. 47
Blame It on My Youth • It's Easy to Remember • June in January • Love Letters • A Nightingale Sang in Berkeley Square • When I Fall in Love • and more.
00843043 ....$14.95

BEBOP CLASSICS Vol. 48
Be-Bop • Bird Feathers • Blue 'N Boogie • Byrd Like • Cool Blues • Dance of the Indifels • Dexterity • Dizzy Atmosphere • Groovin' High • Tempus Fugit.
00843044 ....$14.95

MILES DAVIS STANDARDS Vol. 49
Darn That Dream • I Loves You, Porgy • If I Were a Bell • On Green Dolphin Street • Some Day My Prince Will Come • Yesterdays • and more.
00843045 ....$16.95

GREAT JAZZ CLASSICS Vol. 50
Along Came Betty • Birdland • The Jive Samba • Little Sunflower • Nuages • Peri's Scope • Phase Dance • Road Song • Think on Me • Windows.
00843046 ....$14.95

UP-TEMPO JAZZ Vol. 51
Cherokee (Indian Love Song) • Chi Chi • 52nd Street Theme • Little Willie Leaps • Move • Pent Up House • Topsy • and more.
00843047 ....$14.95

STEVIE WONDER Vol. 52
I Just Called to Say I Love You • Isn't She Lovely • My Cherie Amour • Part Time Lover • Superstition • You Are the Sunshine of My Life • and more.
00843048 ....$14.95

RHYTHM CHANGES Vol. 53
Celia • Chasing the Bird • Cotton Tail • Crazeology • Fox Hunt • I Got Rhythm • No Moe • Oleo • Red Cross • Steeplechase.
00843049 ....$14.95

"MOONLIGHT IN VERMONT" AND OTHER GREAT STANDARDS Vol. 54
A Child Is Born • Love You Madly • Lover Man (Oh, Where Can You Be?) • Moonlight in Vermont • The Night Has a Thousand Eyes • Small Fry • and more.
00843050 ....$14.95

BENNY GOLSON Vol. 55
Along Came Betty • Blues March • Gypsy Jingle-Jangle • I Remember Clifford • Killer Joe • Step Lightly • Whisper Not • and more.
00843052 ....$14.95

VINCE GUARALDI Vol. 57
Blue Charlie Brown • Christmas Time Is Here • Frieda (With the Naturally Curly Hair) • The Great Pumpkin Waltz • Happiness Theme • Linus and Lucy • Oh, Good Grief • The Pebble Beach Theme • Skating • Surfin' Snoopy.
00843057 ....$14.95

MORE LENNON AND McCARTNEY Vol. 58
Can't Buy Me Love • Michelle • Norwegian Wood (This Bird Has Flown) • Eight Days a Week • Yellow Submarine • In My Life • The Long and Winding Road • All My Loving • Julia • Ob-La-Di, Ob-La-Da.
00843059 ....$14.95

SOUL JAZZ Vol. 59
The Cape Verdean Blues • Cold Duck Time • Dat Dere • Freight Trane • Holy Land • The Jive Samba • Nutville • Unit Seven • Work Song.
00843060 ....$14.95

MONGO SANTAMARIA Vol. 61
Afro Blue • Come Candellia • Federico • Las Guajiras • Linda Guajira • Manila • Sabroso • Watermelon Man.
00843062 ....$14.95

JAZZ-ROCK FUSION Vol. 62
Brown Hornet • Chameleon • Got a Match? • Loose Ends • Revelation • Snakes • Spain • Three Views of a Secret • Watermelon Man.
00843063 ....$14.95

CLASSICAL JAZZ Vol. 63
Eine Kleine Nachtmusik • Emperor Waltz • Habanera • Jesu, Joy of Man's Desiring • Minuet in G • New World Symphony (Theme) • Nocturne in F Minor • Ode to Joy • Pavane • Pavane (For a Dead Princess).
00843064 ....$14.95

TV TUNES Vol. 64
Bandstand Boogie • Theme from Family Guy • Theme from Frasier • Hawaii Five-O Theme • Love and Marriage • Mission: Impossible Theme • The Odd Couple • Theme from the Simpsons • Theme from Spider Man • Theme from Star Trek®.
00843065 ....$14.95

SMOOTH JAZZ Vol. 65
Angela • Cast Your Fate to the Wind • Feels So Good • Give Me the Night • Just the Two of Us • Minute by Minute • Morning Dance • Songbird • Street Life • This Masquerade.
00843066 ....$14.95

A CHARLIE BROWN CHRISTMAS Vol. 66
Christmas Is Coming • The Christmas Song (Chestnuts Roasting on an Open Fire) • Christmas Time Is Here • Linus and Lucy • My Little Drum • O Tannenbaum • Skating • What Child Is This.
00843067 ....$14.95

CHICK COREA Vol. 67
Bud Powell • Captain Marvel • 500 Miles High • Litha • The Loop • Mirror, Mirror • Now He Beats the Drum, Now He Stops • (I Can Recall) Spain • Tones for Joan's Bones • Windows.
00843068 ....$14.95

CHARLES MINGUS Vol. 68
Better Get Hit in Your Soul • Boogie Stop Shuffle • Goodbye Pork Pie Hat • Gunslinging Bird • Jelly Roll • Nostalgia in Times Square • Peggy's Blue Skylight • Pithecanthropus Erectus • Portrait • Slippers.
00843069 ....$16.95

CLASSIC JAZZ Vol. 69
Allen's Alley • Detour Ahead • I Wished on the Moon • Let's Get Lost • Nobody Else but Me • Our Delight • Rockin' in Rhythm • A Sleepin' Bee • Soul Eyes • What Is There to Say.
00843071 ....$14.95

THE DOORS Vol. 70
Break on Through to the Other Side • The End • Hello, I Love You (Won't You Tell Me Your Name?) • L.A. Woman • Light My Fire • Love Me Two Times • People Are Strange • Riders on the Storm • Roadhouse Blues • Touch Me.
00843072 ....$14.95

COLE PORTER CLASSICS Vol. 71
Dream Dancing • From This Moment On • I Get a Kick out of You • I Love Paris • I've Got My Eyes on You • Just One of Those Things • Love for Sale • My Heart Belongs to Daddy • Night and Day • What Is This Thing Called Love?
00843073 ....$14.95

CLASSIC JAZZ BALLADS Vol. 72
For Heaven's Sake • Isfahan • Lament • Maybe You'll Be There • The Single Petal of a Rose • Some Other Spring • Sure Thing • Too Young to Go Steady • You're Looking at Me • You've Changed.
00843074 ....$14.95

JAZZ/BLUES Vol. 73
Break Out the Blues • Bremond's Blues • Gee Baby, Ain't I Good to You • I'll Close My Eyes • Movin' Along (Sid's Twelve) • Night Lights • Reunion Blues • The Sermon • Sunny • This Here.
00843075 ....$14.95

0507

Jazz Instruction & Improvisation
Books for All Instruments from Hal Leonard

AN APPROACH TO JAZZ IMPROVISATION
by Dave Pozzi
Musicians Institute Press

INCLUDES TAB

Explore the styles of Charlie Parker, Sonny Rollins, Bud Powell and others with this comprehensive guide to jazz improvisation. Covers: scale choices • chord analysis • phrasing • melodies • harmonic progressions • more.
00695135 Book/CD Pack $17.95

BUILDING A JAZZ VOCABULARY
By Mike Steinel

A valuable resource for learning the basics of jazz from Mike Steinel of the University of North Texas. It covers: the basics of jazz • how to build effective solos • a comprehensive practice routine • and a jazz vocabulary of the masters.
00849911 ....$19.95

THE CYCLE OF FIFTHS
by Emile and Laura De Cosmo

This essential instruction book provides more than 450 exercises, including hundreds of melodic and rhythmic ideas. The book is designed to help improvisors master the cycle of fifths, one of the primary progressions in music. Guaranteed to refine technique, enhance improvisational fluency, and improve sight-reading!
00311114 ....$14.95

THE DIATONIC CYCLE
by Emile and Laura De Cosmo

Renowned jazz educators Emile and Laura De Cosmo provide more than 300 exercises to help improvisors tackle one of music's most common progressions: the diatonic cycle. This book is guaranteed to refine technique, enhance improvisational fluency, and improve sight-reading!
00311115 ....$16.95

EAR TRAINING
by Keith Wyatt,
Carl Schroeder and Joe Elliott
Musicians Institute Press

Covers: basic pitch matching • singing major and minor scales • identifying intervals • transcribing melodies and rhythm • identifying chords and progressions • seventh chords and the blues • modal interchange, chromaticism, modulation • and more.
00695198 Book/2-CD Pack.........................$19.95

EXERCISES AND ETUDES FOR THE JAZZ INSTRUMENTALIST
by J.J. Johnson

Designed as study material and playable by any instrument, these pieces run the gamut of the jazz experience, featuring common and uncommon time signatures and keys, and styles from ballads to funk. They are progressively graded so that both beginners and professionals will be challenged by the demands of this wonderful music.
00842018 Bass Clef Edition.....................$16.95
00842042 Treble Clef Edition $16.95

JAZZOLOGY
THE ENCYCLOPEDIA OF JAZZ THEORY FOR ALL MUSICIANS
by Robert Rawlins and Nor Eddine Bahha

This comprehensive resource covers a variety of jazz topics, for beginners and pros of any instrument. The book serves as an encyclopedia for reference, a thorough methodology for the student, and a workbook for the classroom.
00311167 ....$17.95

JAZZ THEORY RESOURCES
by Bert Ligon
Houston Publishing, Inc.

This is a jazz theory text in two volumes. **Volume 1 includes:** review of basic theory • rhythm in jazz performance • triadic generalization • diatonic harmonic progressions and analysis • substitutions and turnarounds • and more. **Volume 2 includes:** modes and modal frameworks • quartal harmony • extended tertian structures and triadic superimposition • pentatonic applications • coloring "outside" the lines and beyond • and more.
00030458 Volume 1 ....$39.95
00030459 Volume 2 ....$29.95

JOY OF IMPROV
by Dave Frank and John Amaral

This book/CD course on improvisation for all instruments and all styles will help players develop monster musical skills! **Book One** imparts a solid basis in technique, rhythm, chord theory, ear training and improv concepts. **Book Two** explores more advanced chord voicings, chord arranging techniques and more challenging blues and melodic lines. The CD can be used as a listening and play-along tool.
00220005 Book 1 – Book/CD Pack $24.95
00220006 Book 2 – Book/CD Pack $24.95

THE PATH TO JAZZ IMPROVISATION
by Emile and Laura De Cosmo

This fascinating jazz instruction book offers an innovative, scholarly approach to the art of improvisation. It includes in-depth analysis and lessons about: cycle of fifths • diatonic cycle • overtone series • pentatonic scale • harmonic and melodic minor scale • polytonal order of keys • blues and bebop scales • modes • and more.
00310904 ....$14.95

THE SOURCE
THE DICTIONARY OF CONTEMPORARY AND TRADITIONAL SCALES
by Steve Barta

This book serves as an informative guide for people who are looking for good, solid information regarding scales, chords, and how they work together. It provides right and left hand fingerings for scales, chords, and complete inversions. Includes over 20 different scales, each written in all 12 keys.
00240885 ....$12.95

21 BEBOP EXERCISES
by Steve Rawlins

This book/CD pack is both a warm-up collection and a manual for bebop phrasing. Its tasty and sophisticated exercises will help you develop your proficiency with jazz interpretation. It concentrates on practice in all twelve keys – moving higher by half-step – to help develop dexterity and range. The companion CD includes all of the exercises in 12 keys.
00315341 Book/CD Pack.......................$17.95

THE WOODSHEDDING SOURCE BOOK
by Emile De Cosmo

Rehearsing with this method daily will improve technique, reading ability, rhythmic and harmonic vocabulary, eye/finger coordination, endurance, range, theoretical knowledge, and listening skills – all of which lead to superior improvisational skills.
00842000 C Instruments $19.95

FOR MORE INFORMATION, SEE YOUR LOCAL MUSIC DEALER, OR WRITE TO:

HAL•LEONARD® CORPORATION
7777 W. BLUEMOUND RD. P.O. BOX 13819 MILWAUKEE, WI 53213

Prices, contents & availability subject to change without notice.

Visit Hal Leonard online at
www.halleonard.com

ARTIST TRANSCRIPTIONS®

Artist Transcriptions are authentic, note-for-note transcriptions of today's hottest artists in jazz, pop and rock. These outstanding, accurate arrangements are in an easy-to-read format which includes all essential lines. Artist Transcriptions can be used to perform, sequence or for reference.

CLARINET

| 00672423 | Buddy De Franco Collection | $19.95 |

FLUTE

00672379	Eric Dolphy Collection	$19.95
00672372	James Moody Collection – Sax and Flute	$19.95
00660108	James Newton – Improvising Flute	$14.95
00672455	Lew Tabackin Collection	$19.95

GUITAR & BASS

00660113	The Guitar Style of George Benson	$14.95
00672331	Ron Carter – Acoustic Bass	$16.95
00660115	Al Di Meola – Friday Night in San Francisco	$14.95
00604043	Al Di Meola – Music, Words, Pictures	$14.95
00673245	Jazz Style of Tal Farlow	$19.95
00672359	Bela Fleck and the Flecktones	$18.95
00699389	Jim Hall – Jazz Guitar Environments	$19.95
00699306	Jim Hall – Exploring Jazz Guitar	$19.95
00672335	Best of Scott Henderson	$24.95
00672356	Jazz Guitar Standards	$19.95
00675536	Wes Montgomery – Guitar Transcriptions	$17.95
00672353	Joe Pass Collection	$18.95
00673216	John Patitucci	$16.95
00672374	Johnny Smith Guitar Solos	$16.95
00672320	Mark Whitfield	$19.95
00672337	Gary Willis Collection	$19.95

PIANO & KEYBOARD

00672338	Monty Alexander Collection	$19.95
00672487	Monty Alexander Plays Standards	$19.95
00672318	Kenny Barron Collection	$22.95
00672520	Count Basie Collection	$19.95
00672364	Warren Bernhardt Collection	$19.95
00672439	Cyrus Chestnut Collection	$19.95
00673242	Billy Childs Collection	$19.95
00672300	Chick Corea – Paint the World	$12.95
00672537	Bill Evans at Town Hall	$16.95
00672425	Bill Evans – Piano Interpretations	$19.95
00672365	Bill Evans – Piano Standards	$19.95
00672510	Bill Evans Trio – Vol. 1: 1959-1961	$24.95
00672511	Bill Evans Trio – Vol. 2: 1962-1965	$24.95
00672512	Bill Evans Trio – Vol. 3: 1968-1974	$24.95
00672513	Bill Evans Trio – Vol. 4: 1979-1980	$24.95
00672329	Benny Green Collection	$19.95
00672486	Vince Guaraldi Collection	$19.95
00672419	Herbie Hancock Collection	$19.95
00672446	Gene Harris Collection	$19.95
00672438	Hampton Hawes	$19.95
00672322	Ahmad Jamal Collection	$22.95
00672476	Brad Mehldau Collection	$19.95

00672390	Thelonious Monk Plays Jazz Standards – Volume 1	$19.95
00672391	Thelonious Monk Plays Jazz Standards – Volume 2	$19.95
00672433	Jelly Roll Morton – The Piano Rolls	$12.95
00672542	Oscar Peterson – Jazz Piano Solos	$14.95
00672544	Oscar Peterson – Originals	$9.95
00672532	Oscar Peterson – Plays Broadway	$19.95
00672531	Oscar Peterson – Plays Duke Ellington	$19.95
00672533	Oscar Peterson – Trios	$24.95
00672543	Oscar Peterson Trio – Canadiana Suite	$7.95
00672534	Very Best of Oscar Peterson	$22.95
00672371	Bud Powell Classics	$19.95
00672376	Bud Powell Collection	$19.95
00672437	André Previn Collection	$19.95
00672507	Gonzalo Rubalcaba Collection	$19.95
00672303	Horace Silver Collection	$19.95
00672316	Art Tatum Collection	$22.95
00672355	Art Tatum Solo Book	$19.95
00672357	Billy Taylor Collection	$24.95
00673215	McCoy Tyner	$16.95
00672321	Cedar Walton Collection	$19.95
00672519	Kenny Werner Collection	$19.95
00672434	Teddy Wilson Collection	$19.95

SAXOPHONE

00673244	Julian "Cannonball" Adderley Collection	$19.95
00673237	Michael Brecker	$19.95
00672429	Michael Brecker Collection	$19.95
00672351	Brecker Brothers... And All Their Jazz	$19.95
00672447	Best of the Brecker Brothers	$19.95
00672315	Benny Carter Plays Standards	$22.95
00672314	Benny Carter Collection	$22.95
00672394	James Carter Collection	$19.95
00672349	John Coltrane Plays Giant Steps	$19.95
00672529	John Coltrane – Giant Steps	$14.95
00672494	John Coltrane – A Love Supreme	$14.95
00672493	John Coltrane Plays "Coltrane Changes"	$19.95
00672453	John Coltrane Plays Standards	$19.95
00673233	John Coltrane Solos	$22.95
00672328	Paul Desmond Collection	$19.95
00672454	Paul Desmond – Standard Time	$19.95
00672379	Eric Dolphy Collection	$19.95
00672530	Kenny Garrett Collection	$19.95
00699375	Stan Getz	$18.95
00672377	Stan Getz – Bossa Novas	$19.95
00672375	Stan Getz – Standards	$17.95
00673254	Great Tenor Sax Solos	$18.95
00672523	Coleman Hawkins Collection	$19.95
00673252	Joe Henderson – Selections from "Lush Life" & "So Near So Far"	$19.95
00672330	Best of Joe Henderson	$22.95

00673239	Best of Kenny G	$19.95
00673229	Kenny G – Breathless	$19.95
00672462	Kenny G – Classics in the Key of G	$19.95
00672485	Kenny G – Faith: A Holiday Album	$14.95
00672373	Kenny G – The Moment	$19.95
00672516	Kenny G – Paradise	$14.95
00672326	Joe Lovano Collection	$19.95
00672498	Jackie McLean Collection	$19.95
00672372	James Moody Collection – Sax and Flute	$19.95
00672416	Frank Morgan Collection	$19.95
00672539	Gerry Mulligan Collection	$19.95
00672352	Charlie Parker Collection	$19.95
00672444	Sonny Rollins Collection	$19.95
00675000	David Sanborn Collection	$16.95
00672528	Bud Shank Collection	$19.95
00672491	New Best of Wayne Shorter	$19.95
00672455	Lew Tabackin Collection	$19.95
00672334	Stanley Turrentine Collection	$19.95
00672524	Lester Young Collection	$19.95

TROMBONE

| 00672332 | J.J. Johnson Collection | $19.95 |
| 00672489 | Steve Turré Collection | $19.95 |

TRUMPET

00672480	Louis Armstrong Collection	$14.95
00672481	Louis Armstrong Plays Standards	$14.95
00672435	Chet Baker Collection	$19.95
00673234	Randy Brecker	$17.95
00672351	Brecker Brothers... And All Their Jazz	$19.95
00672447	Best of the Brecker Brothers	$19.95
00672448	Miles Davis – Originals, Vol. 1	$19.95
00672451	Miles Davis – Originals, Vol. 2	$19.95
00672450	Miles Davis – Standards, Vol. 1	$19.95
00672449	Miles Davis – Standards, Vol. 2	$19.95
00672479	Dizzy Gillespie Collection	$19.95
00673214	Freddie Hubbard	$14.95
00672382	Tom Harrell – Jazz Trumpet	$19.95
00672363	Jazz Trumpet Solos	$9.95
00672506	Chuck Mangione Collection	$19.95
00672525	Arturo Sandoval – Trumpet Evolution	$19.95

FOR MORE INFORMATION, SEE YOUR LOCAL MUSIC DEALER, OR WRITE TO:

HAL•LEONARD® CORPORATION
7777 W. BLUEMOUND RD. P.O. BOX 13819 MILWAUKEE, WI 53213

Visit our web site for a complete listing of our titles with songlists at
www.halleonard.com

Prices and availability subject to change without notice.

0606

Jazz Theory and Technique

COMPREHENSIVE TECHNIQUE FOR JAZZ MUSICIANS – 2ND EDITION

by Bert Ligon

This book is an essential anthology of technical, compositional, and theoretical exercises, with lots of musical examples.

00030455   All Instruments $29.95

CONNECTING CHORDS WITH LINEAR HARMONY

by Bert Ligon

A study of three basic outlines used in jazz improv and composition, based on a study of hundreds of examples from great jazz artists.

00841077 . . . .$35.00

JAZZ THEORY RESOURCES

by Bert Ligon

Volume I includes: review of basic theory, rhythm in jazz performance, basic tonal materials, triadic generalization, diatonic harmonic progressions and harmonic analysis, substitutions and turnarounds, common melodic outlines, and an overview of voicings.

Volume II includes: modes and modal frameworks, quartal harmony, other scales and colors, extended tertian structures and triadic superimposition, pentatonic applications, coloring "outside" the lines and beyond, analysis, and expanding harmonic vocabulary. Appendices on chord/scale relationships, elaborations of static harmony, endings, composing tips, and theory applications are also included.

00030458 Volume 1 . . . .$39.95
00030459 Volume 2 . . . .$29.95

FOR MORE INFORMATION, SEE YOUR LOCAL MUSIC DEALER, OR WRITE TO:

HAL•LEONARD® CORPORATION

7777 W. BLUEMOUND RD. P.O. BOX 13819 MILWAUKEE, WI 53213

Prices, contents, and availability subject to change without notice.

0107